Kaye Umansky's Robin Hood

The Musical

Script

Script by Kaye Umansky
Music by Stephen Chadwick

Illustrations and cover art by Nick Price

A&C Black

INTRODUCTION

This stage musical version of Robin Hood is designed to be performed by upper primary school children. It would also suit lower secondary school children.

Whether you are aiming for simple staging in a small performance area or a more lavish, large-scale production, you need a clear plan to help you get the most from your rehearsals and facilities. The director has overall responsibility. The musical director is in charge of the songs and can double as choreographer and fight scene co-ordinator. You may want to appoint an adult(s) to oversee props, costumes and scenery, involving a team of children 'backstage'. An adult will be needed to operate the CD player. You may also wish to make a copy of the sound effects on a laptop computer for easy access during the performance.

The scenery can be minimal. However, it would be helpful to have several free-standing, easily-transportable trees and bushes that can be arranged differently for scenes taking place in the forest. The most important requirement is space. You will need to allocate space for the dramatic action and dance, the singing chorus, the CD player and sound system and, if you decide to use them, the piano and pianist. Make sure there are clear routes to and from the performance area and, if possible, a pathway through the audience.

Be flexible with the piece and adapt it to suit your circumstances. Good luck, and have fun!

CAST LIST

Robin Hood	*Robin is everything a hero should be. He has style. He has energy, charm and natural swagger. He is, however, a poor archer. He covers up this fact by claiming that the arrows he shoots fly so fast that they are invisible. His fans are happy to go along with this. He has a substantial number of lines and is frequently on stage.*
Allan-a-Dale	*Although determined to write a great song about Robin, his hero, Allan is a terrible musician. His real skill lies in archery, although he is unaware of his ability. He has a large role and is on stage for much of the play.*
Little John	*Little John is tall, of course. He has a moderate speaking part and joins in with the rap.*
Will Scarlett	*A bit of a dandy. Has a moderate speaking part and joins in with the rap.*
Much the Miller	*Faddy about his diet. Has a moderate speaking part and joins in with the rap.*
Friar Tuck	*Kindly and concerned, with a strong social conscience.*
Maid Marion	*A feisty girl with strong views ahead of her time. Sporty and clever, she has a large speaking role and an optional solo singing part.*
The Marionettes	*Five friends of Marion (Alice, Susan, Phoebe, Lizzie and Sarah) who are also unhappy with the role given to them in history.*
The Sheriff of Nottingham	*A bully. Arrogant and cruel, he thinks he can do anything now he has royal backing. He has a substantial number of lines. Boo him: he's bad.*
Prince John	*Greedy, cowardly and stupid, Prince John has a substantial number of lines and provides much of the comedy.*
Lord Chancellor Fishy	*Prince John's chief advisor. He has quite a large role as the straight man to Prince John.*
Mensa	*A Wise Woman. Beneath her cackling Wise Woman act, she is extremely clever and the possessor of sound common sense. Has an optional singing solo.*
The Poor Family	*Consists of mother, father and son ~ Meg, Seth and Little Sammy, who is annoying. All three have small speaking parts.*
The Villagers	*They appear in two scenes. They have several individual lines. There should be at least four (Old Codger, Amos, Beth, Nan), who have a line each, but there can be many more. Two or three can take part in the archery contest.*
King Richard	*A small, thankless role at the very end. Needs a splendid costume to compensate.*
The Guards	*At least seven Guards are needed for Prince John and the Sheriff. Prince John's are non-speaking. Five of the Sheriff's have small speaking roles. One or two can double up as archers in the archery contest.*
The Singing Chorus	*They lead all the songs. The actors on stage join in. If you have particularly talented singers, they can perform a solo.*
The Invisible Horse	*There is one.*

3

PRODUCTION OVERVIEW

TRACK

PROLOGUE

In Sherwood Forest, long ago... Robin meets Allan-a-Dale, a musician and admirer. He asks to join Robin's gang. Robin turns him down because Allan proves to be a surprisingly good archer and will show him up. Robin confides in the audience.

ON STAGE:
Robin, Allan,
The Merry Men, Friar Tuck,
Marion, The Marionettes, Mensa,
The Poor Family, The Villagers

PROPS:
Allan's guitar, Robin's bow and
quiver of arrows

1-4

SONGS:
What Once was Merrie
Englande, merging into
Twang!, ending with a
twang sound effect

SOUND EFFECTS:
a twang and a thunk
(twice)

MUSIC/ SOUND
EFFECTS:
scene change prologue-1
ending with a fanfare

SCENE 1

Prince John's throne room. Prince John converses with Lord Chancellor Fishy. The Sheriff of Nottingham is given a badge. Prince John tells the Sheriff to tax the people more harshly.

ON STAGE:
Prince John, Lord Chancellor
Fishy, Prince John's Guards, The
Sheriff of Nottingham

PROPS:
Prince John's throne, a long list,
a box of Evil Deed Badges of
increasing size and gaudiness

5-6

SONG:
The Sheriff of
Nottingham

MUSIC:
scene change 1-2

SCENE 2

Maid Marion's garden. We meet Marion's friends (the Marionettes) and Marion herself. They discuss Robin and the role of women in medieval society.

ON STAGE:
Allan, The Marionettes (Alice,
Susan, Phoebe, Lizzie and Sarah),
Maid Marion

PROPS:
Allan's guitar, a small easel with
painting materials, knitting needles
and wool, a water bottle, a backpack
with a box of cakes inside

7-8

SONG:
Medieval Girls

MUSIC:
scene change 2-3

SCENE 3

The village. We meet the villagers and the Poor family. The Sheriff arrives with his men and announces another tax day. The Poors are arrested. Friar Tuck attempts to intervene, with no success.

ON STAGE:
Allan, The Villagers (including Old
Codger, Amos, Beth, Nan), Seth
Poor, Meg Poor, Little Sammy
Poor, The Sheriff, Five Guards,
Friar Tuck

PROPS:
Allan's guitar, a sign saying: 'Little
Mudwallow-In-The-Mire' or
similar, a baby, a boot and hammer,
a patched garment for mending, a
half woven basket, a big cudgel for
the Sheriff, sticks for the Guards,
Sheriff's badge

9

MUSIC/ SOUND
EFFECTS:
scene change 3-4 ending
with a sound effect of
thunder

SCENE 4

ON STAGE:
Mensa, Marion, The Marionettes

PROPS:
a cauldron and stirring stick, a wild grey wig, empty jars, a box of cakes

10

SOUND EFFECTS/ MUSIC:
roll of thunder and scene change 4-5

Mensa's house. Mensa is boiling mice in a cauldron. Marion and the Marionettes visit with some cakes. They talk about Robin and Prince John. Mensa says that she has a plan to flush out Prince John. She gives Marion a cryptic message for Robin.

SCENE 5

ON STAGE:
Allan, The Merry Men, Robin, Maid Marion, The Marionettes, Friar Tuck

PROPS:
a pot of forest stew over an open fire, a jug of apple juice and four tankards, cut-out tree to hide behind, bows and arrows for Robin and his men, Allan's guitar

11-14

SONG:
The Merry Men Rap

SOUND EFFECTS:
horse sound effect (twice), wind blowing tumbleweed

MUSIC:
scene change 5-6 ending with horse sound effect

Robin's camp. Robin and the Merry Men are celebrating a successful robbery, including that of a horse. Marion and the Marionettes arrive. Marion passes on Mensa's message. Friar Tuck arrives with the news about the Poor family's arrest.

SCENE 6

ON STAGE:
Robin, the Merry Men, Friar Tuck, Allan, five Guards, The Poor Family

PROPS:
sticks for Robin, Friar Tuck and the Merry Men, Allan's guitar, cut-out trees/bushes to hide behind, sticks for the Guards

15-17

SONG:
Ambush song

SOUND EFFECTS:
horse sound effect

MUSIC:
scene change 6-7 ending with a fanfare for Prince John

The Ambush. Robin and his men ambush the guards in a forest glade and rescue the Poor family. Allan disgraces himself.

SCENE 7

ON STAGE:
Prince John, his Guards, The Sheriff, Lord Chancellor Fishy, Mensa

PROPS:
John's throne, a basket full of jars containing boiled mice, a splendid silver jar (only used for royalty)

18-21

SONG:
Time to be Hypnotised

SOUND EFFECTS:
thunder (twice)

MUSIC:
scene change 7-8

Prince John's throne room. The Sheriff tells Prince John about Robin's ambush. Fishy brings in Mensa who hypnotises them and plants the idea of holding an archery contest. All three come up with the same suggestion.

5

SCENE 8

Robin's camp. Friar Tuck arrives with news of the archery contest. Mensa's offstage voice reminds Robin to 'Read Between The Lines' – but it is Marion who understands this. They discuss what should be done.

ON STAGE:
Allan, Robin, The Merry Men, Marion, The Marionettes, Friar Tuck, Mensa (offstage)

PROPS:
Allan's guitar, a cut-out bush to hide behind, a sheet of parchment, forest stew over fire

22–26

SOUND EFFECTS:
horse sound effect, thunder, wind blowing tumbleweed (twice)

MUSIC:
scene change 8-9 ending with a fanfare for Prince John

SCENE 9

The contest. Everyone assembles on stage for the archery contest. Prince John receives an unenthusiastic welcome. After a poor display of skill from the contestants, Allan, disguised as 'Old Kevin' hits the bull's-eye. Allan is awarded the golden arrow, Prince John's treasure chest is stolen by Marion and the Marionettes and, finally, King Richard arrives to bring about a happy ending.

ON STAGE:
Prince John, Lord Chancellor Fishy, Prince John's Guards, The Villagers, The Poor Family, Mensa, Maid Marion, the Marionettes, Little John, Will, Much, Friar Tuck, Sheriff's Guards (doubling as archers), The Sheriff, Allan in disguise as 'Old Kevin', Robin, King Richard

PROPS:
a large, brimming treasure chest, carried on a stretcher, Prince John's podium/fancy chair, an umbrella, a target (with arrow to attach to the bull's-eye), small flags for the villagers to wave, bows and arrows for the competing archers, a golden arrow, Allan's guitar, a bunch of flowers

27–34

SONGS:
He's Rich (parts 1 & 2), The Arrow's in the Air (Parts 1 & 2), Twang! (Reprise), ending with a twang sound effect

SOUND EFFECTS/ MUSIC:
King Richard's fanfare, followed by kingly music, horse sound effect

STAGING SUGGESTIONS

There are ten scenes. Seven require a lot of space, three require a small acting area. If you are using a proscenium stage, smaller scenes can take place in front of the curtain. Ideally, it would be good to have two acting areas – the main stage and a smaller stage built of rostra blocks. If you wish to keep scenery to a minimum, you could have a child walking on with a sign to indicate the location, e.g. Maid Marion's Garden, for scene 2. You will need a clear route through the audience for the Prologue and Scene 9.

BACKDROPS

These are not essential. However, it would be good to have a backdrop depicting Sherwood Forest as many of the scenes take place here. If you have a smaller acting area, this doubles as Prince John's throne room (throne required) and Mensa's hut (cauldron required). The backdrop can be plain for these scenes and the set dressed with additional props. Three or four freestanding trees/bushes can be brought on and off as required. If you wish, you could make a freestanding hut to depict the village – although a sign reading 'Little Mudwallow-In-The Mire' would do the trick.

LARGE PROPS

These can be brought on and off by stage hands (who may like to wear medieval costumes). The only essential large props are a throne for Prince John, several freestanding trees/bushes, a cauldron, and a fire with a pot of forest stew to denote Robin's den. It has been suggested that Prince John will sit in a podium during the final scene, but this is not necessary – a fancy chair with an umbrella held by a guard will do just fine. Some flags and pennants would lend a festive air.

COSTUME IDEAS

The costumes can be as simple or elaborate as you wish. Tights and jerkins would be appropriate for Robin and his Merry Men. The female villagers can wear simple skirts, blouses and shawls, with headscarves. The men can wear rough jackets, boots and trousers.

Robin

A green tunic with matching tights. A hat with a feather. He carries his bow and arrows at all times.

Allan-a-Dale

A bit of a medieval hippy. Maybe a headband and beads. Always has his guitar.

Maid Marion

In all scenes but the last one, where she wears a dress, Marion is dressed in a 'medieval jogging outfit' which can be interpreted as you will. It could be a loose, shortish green skirt with a jerkin. She has a green backpack and initially carries a flask of water.

Prince John

A flashy dresser. Elaborate robe, crown, and dripping with jewelry.

The Sheriff of Nottingham

He is described as 'that big, shouty, beardy chap in spikes'. He should be dressed all in black, with a studded belt (holding a dagger) and spikes wherever spikes can go.

Lord Chancellor Fishy

A sober robe, as befits his status. Maybe a beard.

Mensa

Black, ragged clothes and a spectacular wig of wild grey hair.

Little Sammy

Ragged clothes and bare feet. He could carry a medieval teddy.

Merry Men

Tights and jerkins, and again, always armed with bows and arrows. Will Scarlett is a bit of a dandy, and wears red.

Friar Tuck

A plain brown habit and sandals.

Allan's 'Old Kevin' disguise

A hooded cloak with a false beard. Could carry a staff to aid walking.

The Marionettes

Traditional medieval gowns in varying colours, possibly with wimples.

The Guards

Dressed in armour. Prince John's Guards could have swords. The Sheriff's Guards require sticks. Prince John's Guards and the Sheriff's men should be differentiated by their costumes ~ grander for Prince John's Guards; that's only fair, because they never speak.

King Richard

Has a splendid costume to make up for having such a small part.

The Singing Chorus

Can be dressed in Lincoln Green. Maybe green hats with feathers.

The Horse

It's invisible.

THE SCRIPT

PROLOGUE ~ IN SHERWOOD FOREST, LONG AGO…

Allan-a-Dale sits beneath a tree to the side, hunched over his guitar.

SONG ~ WHAT ONCE WAS MERRIE ENGLANDE / TWANG!

> *All:*
> **What once was Merrie Englande is merrie now
>   no more.
> King Richard has departed to fight a distant war.
> A land now doomed to silence where once glad
>   voices rang.
> But have no fear! For who comes here,
> With his easy grin and his flash green gear?**

Change of mood. Robin, the Merry Men, Marion, the Marionettes, Friar Tuck, the Poor Family, Mensa and the Villagers parade onto the stage, singing. Robin poses centre stage with his bow. Allan remains frozen outside the action.

> *Chorus*
> **He's the guy who goes twang! Twang!
> He's the guy who goes twang! Twang-a-lang!
> He's the guy who goes twang! Twang!
> He's the guy who goes twang! Twang-a-lang!**
>
> **And he lived long ago with an arrow and bow,
> In an outlaw gang! [What a gang!]
> He wore a suit of lovely Lincoln Green,
> Like a medieval model in a magazine.
> That dude called Robin Hood,
> He's the guy who goes twang-a-lang!
> The guy who goes twang!**
>
> **And all the girls say, 'Hey! There goes a boy
>   with style,
> Got a hat with a feather and a real cute smile.'
> All the boys say, 'Hey man! We can be like him,
> If we spend more time down at the gym!'**
>
> *Chorus*
> **He's the guy who goes twang! Twang!...**

10

He can swing through the trees with the greatest
    of ease,
Like an orang-utan! [Orang-utan!]
He wore a suit of lovely Lincoln Green,
Like a medieval model in a magazine.
That dude called Robin Hood,
He's the guy who goes twang-a-lang!
The guy who goes twang!

So just sit back while we tell you what you need
    to know,
About the dude in the wood with the arrow
    and bow,
It's a fact that a show should begin with a bang,
But our show begins with a simple twang, oh yeah!
Yes, our show begins with a simple twang!

In time with the twang sound effect at the end of the song, Robin draws a [non-existent] arrow from his quiver faster than the eye can see and lets fly. Such is his style and confidence that the watching cast are completely taken in, convinced that he shot a real arrow. They follow its imaginary arc.

All: Woooooooooooow!

Merry Men: Go, Robin!

Marion: That's my boy!

Music. Exit everyone, apart from Robin and Allan. Allan instantly comes to life. He is attempting to write a song, but is a dreadful musician. He strums discords and sings tunelessly, with pauses for thought. Robin is still holding his pose.

Allan: *[sings]* I am a wandering minstrel, I roam from town to town… *[strums discord]*

Robin: Right. That's enough posing for one day. Need to rest my bow arm.

Allan: I dumdy dumdy something… I wear a lot of brown…

Robin: *[notices Allan]* Hey! What have we here? Some sort of hippy?

He strides up to Allan.

Robin: What's that you're playing, friend?

Allan: Why, it's called folk music, stranger. It belongs to the common people.

Robin: What ~ they want it?

Allan: Certainly. You can take their money and the bread from their mouths, but you can't take away their music. *[strums discordantly]*

Robin: Mm. Me, I'm more of a hip hop guy. What's your name, friend?

11 Forward to next track

11

Allan:	They call me Allan-a-Dale.
Robin:	Yeah? Well, they call me Robin Hood. Well met!

Robin attempts a high five. Allan fails to respond. He is in a state of shock.

Allan:	Did you say ~ Robin Hood? *The* Robin Hood?
Robin:	Yep, that's me.
Allan:	But ~ this is amazing! I'm a huge fan! I've got all your Wanted posters.
Robin:	Yeah, they don't stay up long. Especially the signed ones.
Allan:	Oh, this is my lucky day! You're the talk of Nottingham! Everyone knows about you and your gang. How you take from the greedy and give to the needy.
Robin:	Yep. I take it you approve?
Allan:	Approve? You're my inspiration! In fact, now we've met, I'm going to write a song about you! Tell your story to the world!
Robin:	You are?
Allan:	I am! I'm a bard, it's what I do! With your fame and my musical talent, we could go places! We could have a hit!
Robin:	Well, er ~ okay. Try to make it upbeat.
Allan:	Any chance of me joining the gang? As official songwriter?
Robin:	Mm. How good are you with a bow?
Allan:	I don't know. Music is my weapon.
Robin:	Well, I guess you can do a fair bit of damage with that. It's not enough, though. You have to shoot straight.
Allan:	I could give it a try.
Robin:	Here. Careful, the arrows are sharp.

Robin hands over his bow and quiver and watches with a grin while Allan fumbles inexpertly.
He nearly strangles himself with the quiver, drops the arrow, fits it facing the wrong way, etc.

Allan:	Sorry. Won't be a minute. Hang on. Oops, wrong way round, silly me...

Finally, he is organised, arrow in place.

Robin:	Ready to rumble?
Allan:	Yes, I think so.
Robin:	*[pointing offstage]* See that tall tree over there, in the distance? Aim for the top branch.

Allan: *[sighting the arrow]* Right. Here goes.

Build-up music plays as Allan fires the arrow offstage followed by the sound effect of a twang and a thunk. Shocked pause.

Forward to next track

Robin: Good grief! You hit it! *[Rubs eyes in astonishment.]*

Allan: *[peering]* Oh. So I did. Beginner's luck, I guess.

Robin: Try again.

Build-up music plays as Allan does it again followed by the sound effect of a twang and a thunk.

Forward to next track

Robin: I don't believe it. The second arrow's split the first.

Allan: Oh, no! What have I done?

Robin: *[still dazed and gazing offstage]* What?

Allan: I've ruined your arrow. I'm so, so sorry. I suppose that means I can't join the gang. Oh, what an idiot. *[Slumps dejectedly, head in hands.]*

Robin: *[to audience]* I've never seen anything like it. He's a natural. This is tricky. You don't know what I'm talking about, do you? Can you keep a secret? *[moves centre stage and confides in the audience]* Okay, I'll tell you. You think I've got everything it takes to be a hero. The hat, the moves, the green suit, all that. But here's the thing ~ I'm a rubbish archer. The invisible arrow thing's just an invention. The fans play along with it. They don't want to spoil the myth, you see. So I can't hire Allan. He's the real deal. He'll show me up. I'll tell him now. *[to Allan]* Sorry, mate, it's a no.

Allan: I knew you'd say that. I should stick to music. That's what I'm good at.

Robin: Ye-e-e-s. *[Takes back his bow and quiver.]*

Allan: Will you do me a favour? Show me how it's really done. They say your arrows fly so fast, they're invisible. I'd love to see that.

Robin: No, I don't think so, Allan. Not right now.

Allan: Why not?

Robin: No time. Places to go, people to see, wrongs to right. No rest for the hero.

Allan: Oh. Yes, I understand. But where shall I find you when I've finished the song? We need to discuss the split.

Robin: There's a secret camp in the wood, under the old oak tree. Follow the smell of wood smoke. Fare thee well, Allan-a-Dale!

Exit Robin, bounding.

13

Allan: *[to audience]* Can you believe it? I've just met Robin Hood! In the flesh! Shame I messed up the archery, but I'll make up for it by coming up with a really brilliant song. *[to himself]* Now then, what do I need? Parchment and a quill pen! Throat lozenges! Space to be creative! Song writing, here I come.

Allan bustles out excitedly. Linking music to next scene.

Forward to next track

SCENE 1 ~ PRINCE JOHN'S THRONE ROOM

A fanfare is heard. Prince John sits on his throne, yawning.

Prince John: Bored. Bored, bored, bored. Need to buy something. Golden shoes. Golden trousers. Put in golden central heating, this place is freezing. Something. Hmm. What shall it be?

Enter Lord Chancellor Fishy with a long list and a box marked EVIL DEED BADGES.

Prince John: Oh, it's you, Lord Chancellor Fishy. What?

Fishy: Good morning, Prince John. Sleep well?

Prince John: No. Tell cook, no more swan burgers last thing. The royal tummy is distinctly iffy.

Fishy: I'll make a note, sire.

Prince John: What's that list you've got there? I hope I don't have to do something.

Fishy: Just a few matters of state to attend to.

Prince John: Well, make it quick.

Fishy: The usual bunch of protesters is outside, complaining about the rise in taxes. They've handed in a petition.

Prince John: Stick it in the royal lavatory. I hope it's a long one. That swan was a big mistake.

Fishy: A message has arrived from King Richard. He requests that you urgently send him money for the crusades. And socks. He's run out of both, apparently.

Prince John: Ah, bother my brother! Serve him right for running off to war. Hang the messenger, we'll say he never arrived. What else?

Fishy: The new Sheriff of Nottingham is here, asking for his sheriff badge.

Prince John: What? That big, shouty chap in spikes? I don't remember promising him a badge.

Fishy: All sheriffs have badges, sire. It comes with the job.

Prince John: Honestly. Some people. I give him a castle, a decent

wage and permission to go pillaging whenever he likes. What more does he want?

Fishy: A badge.

Prince John: A badge. He wants a badge. Do we have any spare badges lying around?

Fishy: Right here. Shall I call him in?

Prince John: I suppose so.

Fishy: Send in the Sheriff!

Enter the Sheriff. He approaches the throne and bows.

Sheriff: Your Highness.

Prince John: Yes, hello. I hear you're expecting a badge.

Sheriff: Well, yes. Shows that I represent the Law, you know? People respect a badge.

Prince John: More than they respect a big, sharp, scary knife?

Sheriff: Well ~ that too, of course. Heh, heh.

Both laugh unpleasantly.

Prince John: Do the honours, Fishy.

Fishy dips into the box, produces a small badge and passes it to Prince John.

Prince John: Here is your badge, Sheriff. Step up.

Sheriff: That's it? I thought it would be bigger.

Prince John: You did?

Sheriff: Well, yes. You can hardly see it. It should be bigger and badder. That'd be better.

Prince John: *[wearily]* Is there a bigger, badder, better badge, Fishy?

Fishy: I don't know.

Prince John: Well, look! I'd like to get this over with. Anyway, congratulations, Sheriff, you've got the job. You are now the Sheriff of Nottingham!

The Sheriff raises his arms in a gesture of triumph. During the following song, he strides around in a threatening manner while Fishy rummages through the badge box. The Sheriff revels in his wickedness. He encourages the audience to join in with random hissing and booing, cupping his hand to his ear and laughing.

SONG ~ THE SHERIFF OF NOTTINGHAM

Chorus
He's the Sheriff of Nottingham,
He's an absolutely terrifying man.
He's the Sheriff of Nottingham,

15

He's devising a very wicked plan.
His fearsome reputation will be known
　　throughout the nation,
The horrifying things he'll do will make you want
　　to hiss and boo. [Hiss! Boo!]

Sheriff: Music to my ears!

[Hiss! Boo!]

**He will threaten you with axes,
He will double up your taxes,
He will take away your money
And your kiddies' bread and honey too! [Hiss! Boo!]**

Fishy offers a bigger badge. The Sheriff rejects it.

Sheriff: Bigger!

[Hiss! Boo!]

Fishy and Prince John both scrabble anxiously through the box.

**He will make you bow and grovel,
Then set fire to your hovel,
Then go home to dine on shellfish,
For he's greedy and he's selfish too! [Hiss! Boo!]**

A bigger badge is offered by Fishy. Again, this is rejected.

Sheriff: Badder!

[Hiss! Boo!]

More scrabbling through the box. Throughout the rest of the song, a series of badges, increasingly bigger and badder, are offered, all of which are rejected.

Chorus
He's the Sheriff of Nottingham...

An enormous, glittering badge is proffered by Fishy. The Sheriff loves it.

Sheriff: That'll do nicely.

[Hiss! Boo!]

During the final verse, Prince John pins the badge onto the Sheriff's chest.

He is dastardly and doomy,

Sheriff: *[shouted]* Ah, so go ahead and sue me!

**You can whimper all you like,
He'll have your head upon a spike, boo-hoo!
[Hiss! Boo! Hiss! Boo!]
He's the Sheriff of Nottingham. [Hiss! Boo!]
He's the Sheriff of Nottingham. [Hiss! Boo!]**

All:
With a badge!

 Forward to
next track

Prince John:	You'd better prove yourself worthy. I'm banking on you to swell the royal coffers. I am, to all intents and purposes, the king. Kings are big spenders.
Sheriff:	No news of King Richard, then?
Prince John:	None whatsoever. Haven't heard from him for ages. Off you go. Oh ~ do that thing about doubling the taxes.
Fishy:	You've just had a tax day, sire.
Prince John:	Well, I want another one. Got that, Sheriff? A second tax day, by Royal decree.
Sheriff:	What are we taxing this time?
Prince John:	I don't know, make something up. Living in a slum. Possessing nose hairs. Breathing. Anything. Is that a problem?
Sheriff:	Oh, no ~ not now I've got the badge. Ha ha ha ha!

Shakes fist at the audience. Linking music to next scene.

SCENE 2 ~ MAID MARION'S GARDEN

The Marionettes are frozen in a demure tableau. They are knitting, sewing and painting. Allan enters and addresses the audience from the side of the stage.

| Allan: | Here I am again. Finding space to compose is proving difficult. You'd think there'd be loads of quiet glades in Sherwood Forest, but not so. Birds, wolves, noisy waterfalls, they're all conspiring against me. I've just sneaked into Maid Marion's garden hoping for some peace and quiet. I wasn't expecting that lot. *[points to the tableau]* Anyway, let me play you what I've done so far… |

Allan opens his mouth to sing, but is interrupted by the musical introduction to Medieval Girls. The tableau comes to life.

| Allan: | Oh ~ rats! |

Exits, looking disgruntled.

SONG ~ MEDIEVAL GIRLS

Marionettes:
We sit, we knit, we do a little painting,
We do a lot of fiddling with our curls.
We lace our waists and practise dainty fainting;
There's nothing else to do, because we're girls.

Chorus
We're girls, medieval girls,
The ones who all the history books don't mention.
We're girls, medieval girls,

17

The boys get all the action and attention.
We're expected to be meek, we're expected not
to speak,
For our role is just to curtsey and obey.
We're required to be dumb, we are underneath
 the thumb,
And we never ever get to have a say.
We're girls, just girls, medieval girls.

And so, we sit, we knit, we do a little painting,
We do a lot of fiddling with our curls,
We lace our waists and practise dainty fainting,
There's nothing else to do, because we're girls.

Music continues. Enter Marion, armed with a bow and arrow and a bottle of water. She is wearing a medieval jogging outfit and has a small backpack. The Marionettes form a group around her.

Marion: Not so!

Marionettes: Not so?

Marion: Not so!

Marion:
Not so. I know we're always in the shadows,
Us girls are never featured in the tales.
They say we're just a boring bunch of saddos,
Who always take a back seat to the males.

Chorus (all):
We're girls, medieval girls,
The ones who all the history books don't mention.
We're girls, medieval girls,
The boys get all the action and attention.

Marion:
It really makes me mad, yes, it really makes me sad,
That the guys get all the honour and the glory.

All:
It's time to make some noise,
We are up there with the boys
And entitled to a mention in the story.
We're girls, just girls, medieval girls.

And so, although we hardly get a look-in,
As the world's recorded history unfurls,
There's more to us than washing up and cooking,
It's time to take a stand for all the girls!

Chorus
We're girls, medieval girls,...

We're girls, just girls, medieval girls!

Forward to
next track

18

Marion:	Let's hear it for the girls!
All girls:	Hooray!
Marion:	Right. I don't want to hear any more silly nonsense about fainting. Who's coming for a jog in the woods?
Alice:	What ~ now?
Susan:	We're not really dressed for jogging.
Marion:	Oh come on, it'll do you good.
Lizzie:	You're just hoping you'll bump into Robin.
Marion:	I'm not. I'm going to drop off a few cakes to Mother Mensa.
Susan:	What ~ the Wise Woman?
Phoebe:	She's scary!
Lizzie:	She's got an evil eye!
Sarah:	And evil ears!
Alice:	They say she can see into the future.
Marion:	Rubbish. She's perfectly harmless and extremely sensible.
Phoebe:	And her hut just happens to be near Robin's den.
Lizzie:	I don't know what your father would say if he knew you were friends with a common outlaw... who does bad stuff.
Marion:	He doesn't do bad stuff. Little bit of trespass. Teeny bit of light poaching. What's so bad about that?
Sarah:	I heard that he robbed another banker only this morning.
Alice:	Three bags of gold, and a horse. The banker's furious.
Susan:	He's complained to the new Sheriff of Nottingham.
Phoebe:	Robin's number one on the Sheriff's blacklist, they say.
Marion:	Well, he shouldn't be. It's not as if he keeps the money. He takes it from those who won't miss it and gives it to people who need it.
Lizzie:	She has a point, you know.
Marion:	Of course I do. Now, are you coming or shall I go on my own?
Sarah:	Okay, okay, we'll come.
Marion:	That's more like it. Ready? Hup, 2, 3, 4...

Exit Marion and the Marionettes, jogging. Linking music to next scene.

19

SCENE 3 ~ THE VILLAGE

Forward to
next track

Women mend clothing and weave baskets. A woman cradles a baby. A cobbler hammers nails into an old shoe. Everyone seems tired and depressed. Enter Allan. He speaks from the side of the stage in hushed, narrator's tones.

Allan: Well, here we are at the village. What a depressing scene. It's hard to relax when you owe a lot of tax. Hey, that's a good line. I'll use it in the song. I'm getting on quite well with it, actually. This is what I've done so far.

Allan strums his discord and opens his mouth to sing, but is interrupted by the entrance of Little Sammy Poor.

Little Sammy: Mummy, mummy! There's a big bad man coming, with soldiers!

Allan: I don't believe it.

Exit Allan, disconsolate. Much consternation from the Villagers, who form fearful huddles. Enter the armed, black-cloaked Sheriff, with five stick-wielding Guards.

Sheriff: All right, you scum, listen up. I'm the new Sheriff of Nottingham. I'm here to collect your taxes.

Old Codger: Where's your badge?

Sheriff: *[whisking back his cloak to display badge]* Right here, Old Codger. Get a load of that.

Seth: But we've already paid. Tax day was last month.

Sheriff: This is another one. Orders of Prince John.

Meg: He can't do that! He's not the king! King Richard is!

Seth: We're all cleaned out! We can't pay again. This isn't fair!

Sheriff: Guards, arrest that woman for treason and that man for tax avoidance.

The Guards seize Meg and Seth. More panic from the Villagers.

Villagers: No! Stop! You can't do that!

Seth: *[struggling]* Leave my wife alone!

Little Sammy: Mummy! Don't hurt my mummy, you naughty man!

Sheriff: Take the kid too. He's really annoying.

Enter Friar Tuck.

Friar Tuck: What's going on here?

Amos: He's arresting them for treason!

Beth: He says we have to pay more taxes!

Nan: Help us, Friar!

Friar Tuck: *[to the Sheriff]* You can't do this! There's such a thing as human rights!

Sheriff: Not yet, there isn't. Take 'em to Nottingham, boys, and throw 'em in the slammer.

Friar Tuck: This is an outrage! I protest!

Sheriff: Friar Tuck, isn't it? I've heard about you.

Friar Tuck: These people are innocent! Since when has poverty been a crime? How can they give what they don't have?

Sheriff: You'd be surprised what they find under the mattress when their hut's on fire. Take 'em away, boys. Any more interference from you, Tuck, and you'll be banged up with 'em. So be warned.

The Guards roughly push the Poors and Friar Tuck offstage.

Friar Tuck: Get your hands off me…

Sheriff: The rest of you, stand back. I'm conducting a hovel to hovel search, with a big, flaming torch. *[to audience]* That's the sort of thing you can do when you've got a badge.

Linking music to next scene ending with a sound effect of thunder.

SCENE 4 ~ MENSA'S HOUSE

Mensa sits, stirring a cauldron. A wig of wild grey hair hangs on her chair.

Mensa: *[singing]* Mice are nice in a cauldron, a cauldron, a cauldron…

Marion: *[offstage]* Hello? Anyone in?

Mensa: Ooh! A customer! *[Hastily stands and puts on the wig. Adopts a scary voice]* Who dares call upon the Wise Woman?

Marion: It's only us. Marion and the girls.

Mensa: *[in a normal voice]* Oh, Marion. Push on the door, dear, it's open.

Enter Marion and the Marionettes, huffing and puffing.

Marion: Hello, Mother Mensa. I've brought you some cakes.

Mensa: You have? Well, that's very kind.

Marion: I'm scared you're not eating properly, living here all alone. You don't even have a phone.

Mensa: It's the Middle Ages, dear ~ nobody does.

Alice: I'd like one, though.

Susan: You don't know what one is.

21

Alice:	I'd still like one.
Marion:	No point, you can't ring anybody. *[to Mensa]* You can take the wig off now.
Mensa:	I will. Itches like the devil, it do. *[removes wig]* That's better.
Phoebe:	*[sniffs]* What are you cooking?
Mensa:	Oh, you know me. Whatever's in me cupboard.
Marion:	The last time I looked, there were only mice in your cupboard.
Mensa:	Exactly. *[cackles gleefully]* Oh, lighten up, I'm not eatin' 'em. I'm just boilin' 'em up to put in jars. For me mystic readin's.

Marion takes a box of cakes from her backpack and hands it to Mensa.

Marion:	Here. Medieval muffins. They've got apple in. One of your five a day.
Mensa:	My favourite! You're a good girl, you are. I don't suppose you thought to bring the cryptic crossword from the Medieval Times?
Marion:	No, sorry.
Mensa:	No worries. Too easy anyway. I solves it faster than I can fill it in. So. Anythin' I can do for you girls while you're here? Any equations need solvin'? Brief explanation of rocket science? Stuck on the Sudoku?
Lizzie:	Not today, thanks.
Mensa:	Anyone want to be hypnotised? For a giggle?
Sarah:	Not right now. We're on a jog, you see.
Mensa:	Will you be passin' by Robin's den, by any chance?
Marion:	Well, yes. Probably.
Mensa:	How is he these days?
Marion:	Oh, fine. Just fine.
Lizzie:	She's worried he'll get caught.
Alice:	The news is there's a new sheriff. And he's nasty.
Susan:	He'll want to make a name for himself.
Phoebe:	Prince John's given him sweeping new powers.
Mensa:	That Prince John. Holed up in his castle. Dishin' out his orders. Too scared to face the common folk. They'll rise up and do for him once they see him lordin' it around.

Kaye Umansky's Robin Hood

The Musical

Score

Script by Kaye Umansky
Music by Stephen Chadwick
A&C Black

First published 2013 by A & C Black, an imprint of Bloomsbury Publishing Plc, 50 Bedford Square, London WC1B 3DP
ISBN 978-1-4081-9309-5
Text of Kaye Umansky's Robin Hood © 2013 Kaye Umansky
The Arrow's in the Air (parts 1 & 2) lyrics © 2013 Stephen Chadwick
All other lyrics for Kaye Umanksy's Robin Hood © 2013 Kaye Umansky
Original songs, musical arrangements and incidental music © Stephen Chadwick

CUE:	SINGERS:
(Use this space to write your own reminder of the action which precedes the song)	ALL

What Once was Merrie Englande / Twang!

28
guy who goes twang! Twang-a-lang!__
1. And he lived long ago with an
2. He can swing through the trees with the

31
ar-row and bow,_____ In an out-law gang! (What a gang!) He wore a
great-est of ease,_ Like an o-rang-u-tan! (O-rang-u-tan!)_ He wore a

34
suit of love-ly Lin-coln Green,_ Like a med-i-e-val mod-el in a

37
mag-a-zine.__ That dude called Rob-in Hood,___ He's the

guy who goes twang - a - lang! The guy who goes twang!

And all the girls say, 'Hey!
So just sit back while we tell you

There goes a boy with
what you need to

style,
know,

Got a hat with a fea - ther
A - bout the dude in the wood

and a real cute smile',
with the ar row and bow,

All the boys say, 'Hey man!
It's a fact that a show should

We can be   like   him,   If we spend more time
be - gin___ with a bang,   But   our   show be - gins

down   at the   gym!"   He's the

with a sim - ple twang,   oh yeah! Yes,

our   show be - gins   with a sim - ple twang!

The Sheriff of Nottingham

Medieval Girls

-pect-ed to be meek,___ we're ex-pect-ed not to speak,___ For our
real-ly makes me mad,___ yes, it real-ly makes me sad,___ That the

All: (every time)

role is just to curt-sey and o-bey. We're re-quir-ed to be dumb, we are
guys get all the ho-nour and the glo-ry. It's time to make some noise, We are

un-der-neath___ the thumb, And we nev-er ev-er get to have a
up there with the boys___ And en-ti-tled to a men-tion in the

3rd time to Coda

say. We're girls, just girls, med-i-e-val
sto-ry.

CUE:	SINGERS:
(Use this space to write your own reminder of the action which precedes the song)	ALL (except Robin Hood) RAP: WILL, LITTLE JOHN and MUCH

The Merry Men Rap

Rap

1. **Will** [rapped]: This is the den of the ...
2. **Much** [rapped]: Now listen up and have some ...
3. **The Merry Men** perform tough moves and poses etc. as the choir performs the chant and vocal sounds.

KAYE UMANSKY'S ROBIN HOOD THE MUSICAL © 2013 A&C BLACK PUBLISHERS LTD

Chorus: All

work for Rob, do a real good job, the best that we can do,___ We're

big and strong, we right the wrong,_ we live on for - est stew,_ We

Repeat twice

laugh and sing like a - ny -thing, You are look-in' at the cho - sen few._

This is the den of the Migh-ty Mer-ry Men, You are look-in' at the cho-sen few.__

mf

Ambush Song

♩ = 144

Chorus 1: Merry Men:

Let the fight be - gin! We can't wait for it! Wipe the floor with you, knock you round a bit!

Verse 1: Merry Men only
Verse 2: Guards only

Run a - long_____ back to your mo - thers,
Though we come_____ a - cross as yobs,_____ guv,

Hide be-hind_____ your ba-by bro - thers, We
Bear in mind_____ there ain't no jobs,_____ guv. Oh

know our_ fight-ing is su - pe - ri - or,_____ And
please show us mer - cy, let us run a - way,_____ And

we can't_ wait____ to knock you down!
we'll head_ for_____some far - off town.

1.

***Chorus 2*: Guards only**

mp

Please don't_ hurt_____ us! Please don't_ blame_____ us!

mp

Choruses 1 and 2 together:

Was - n't___ our___ fault, some - one_ made___ us!

Let the fight be - gin! We can't wait for it!

Please don't_ hurt___ us! Please don't_ blame___ us!

2nd time to Coda

Wipe the floor with you, knock you round a bit!

Was - n't__ our___ fault, some - one_ made___ us!

Greensleeves chase instrumental

D. S. al Coda

Coda

Time to be Hypnotised

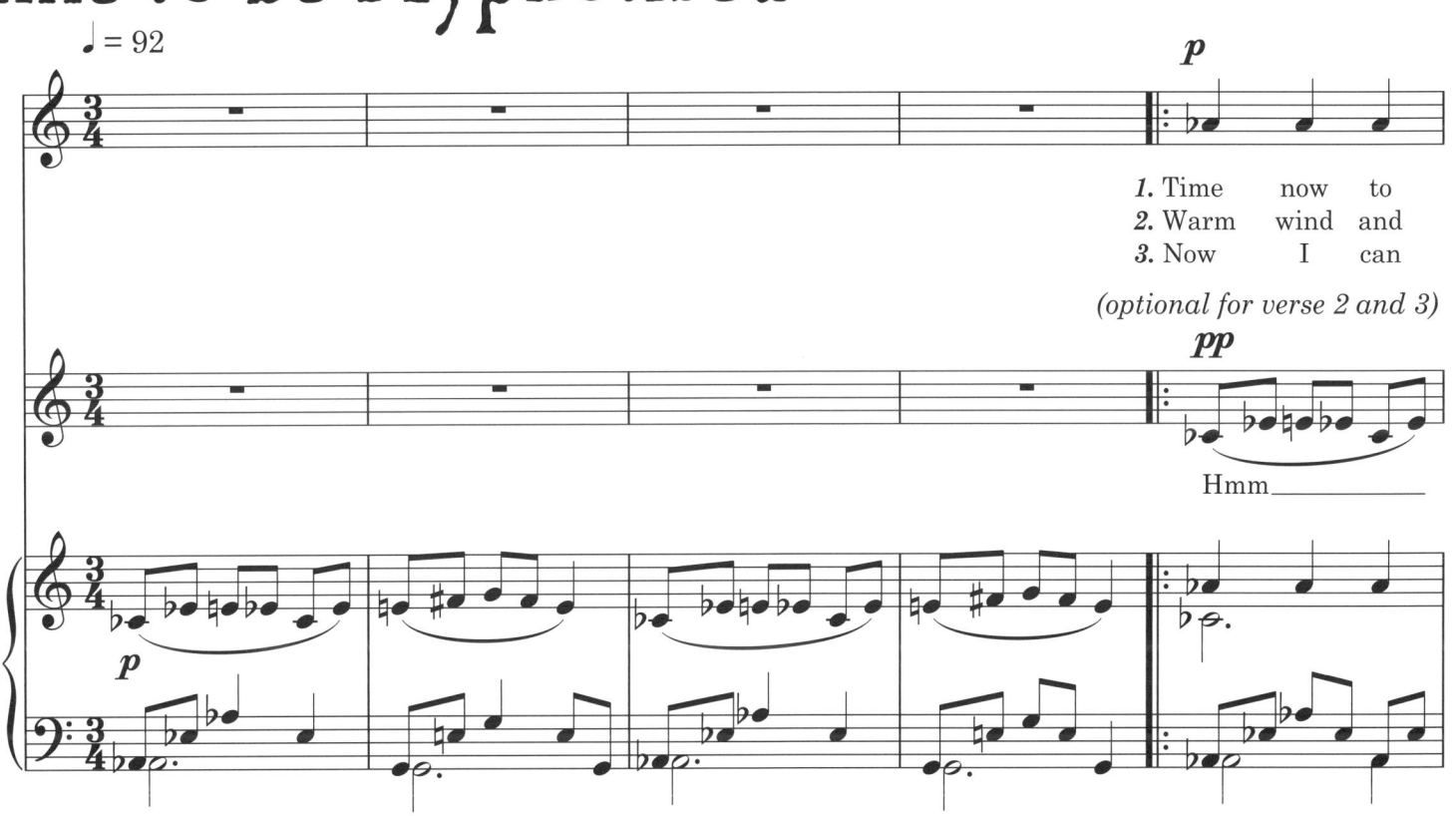

1. Time now to
2. Warm wind and
3. Now I can

(optional for verse 2 and 3)

Hmm

close your eyes,   time to be   hyp - no - tised.   All now will be re - vealed,
sky of blue,   ev - 'ry - one   lov - ing you,   Ev - 'ry - one cheer - ing you,
clear - ly see,   a con - test of   ar - cher - y.   Here in your hand you hold,   an

Ahh   Hmm   Ahh   Hmm   Ahh

He's Rich (parts 1 & 2)

stink - ing, stink - ing rich!

Part 1 His trea - sure chest is full to o - ver-
Part 2 You've nev - er ev - er seen a man so

rich, rich, rich, rich, rich!

- flow - ing,_____ He's rich! Prince John is rich! He's
greed - y,_____ He's rich! Prince John is rich! He's

Rich, rich, rich, rich, rich, rich, rich, rich,

stink - ing, stink - ing rich! How rich he is, we have no way of
stink - ing, stink - ing rich! He does - n't give a fig a - bout the

rich, rich, rich, rich, rich!

know-ing,_____ He's rich! Prince John is rich! His
need-y,_____ He's rich! Prince John is rich! We

Rich, rich, rich, rich, rich!

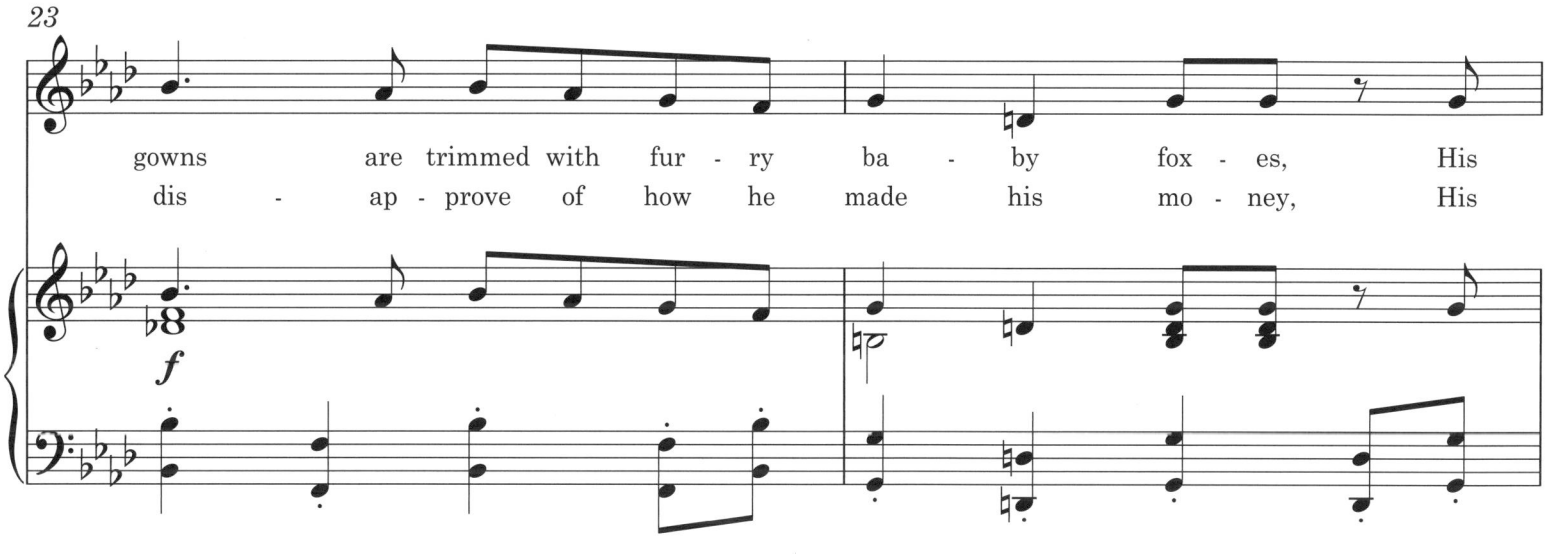

gowns are trimmed with fur-ry ba-by fox-es, His
dis - ap-prove of how he made his mo-ney, His

crowns are al-ways spill-ing out of box-es, He's loads of gold and je-wels
ruth - less me-thods aren't the least bit fun-ny, He'll be ex-pect-ing us to

First time continue
For Part 2 ending go to bar 39

by the score, But he's al - ways want - ing more and more, } He's
clap and cheer, But he'll get a poor re - cep - tion here, }

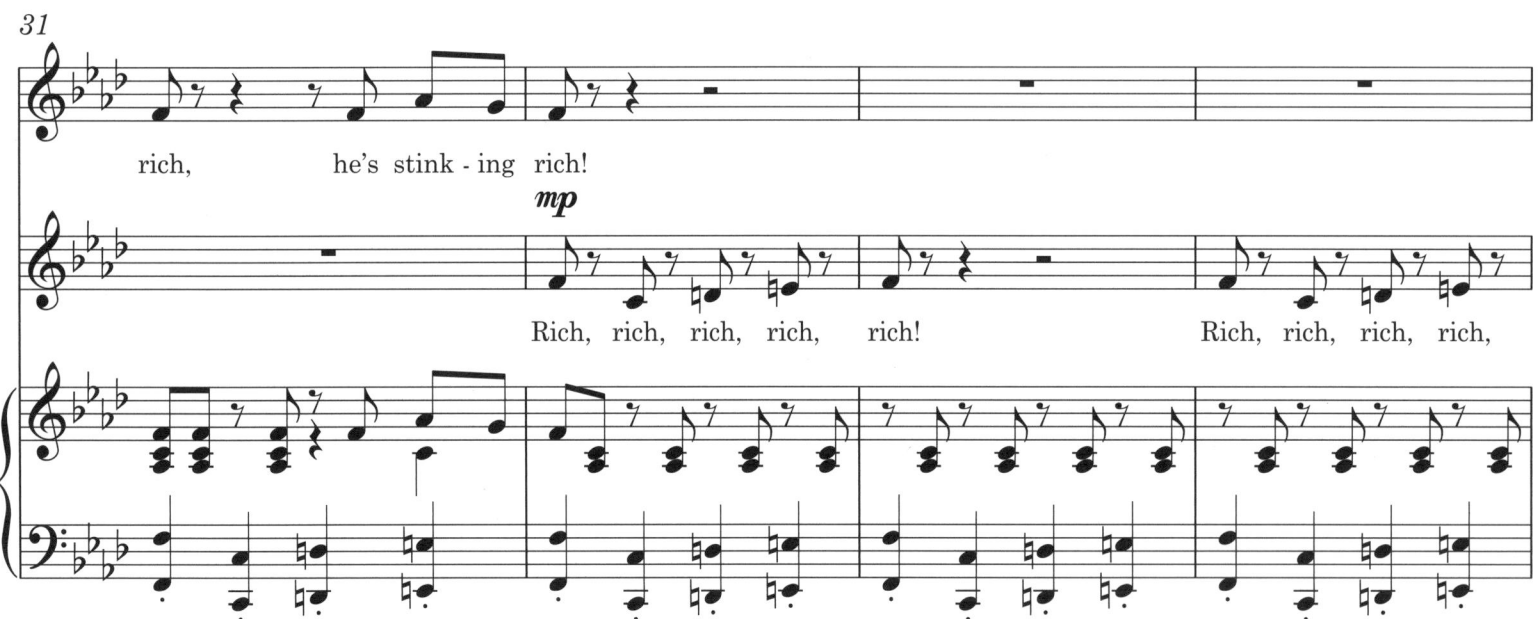

rich, he's stink - ing rich!

Rich, rich, rich, rich, rich! Rich, rich, rich, rich,

End of Part 1

rich! Rich, rich, rich, rich, rich, rich, rich, rich.

28

Part 2 ending

CUE:	SINGERS:
(Use this space to write your own reminder of the action which precedes the song)	ALL

The Arrow's in the Air (parts 1 & 2)

Part 1 continue
For Part 2 ending go to bar 34

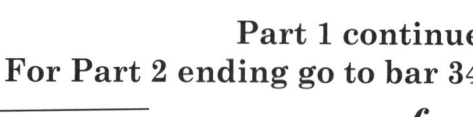

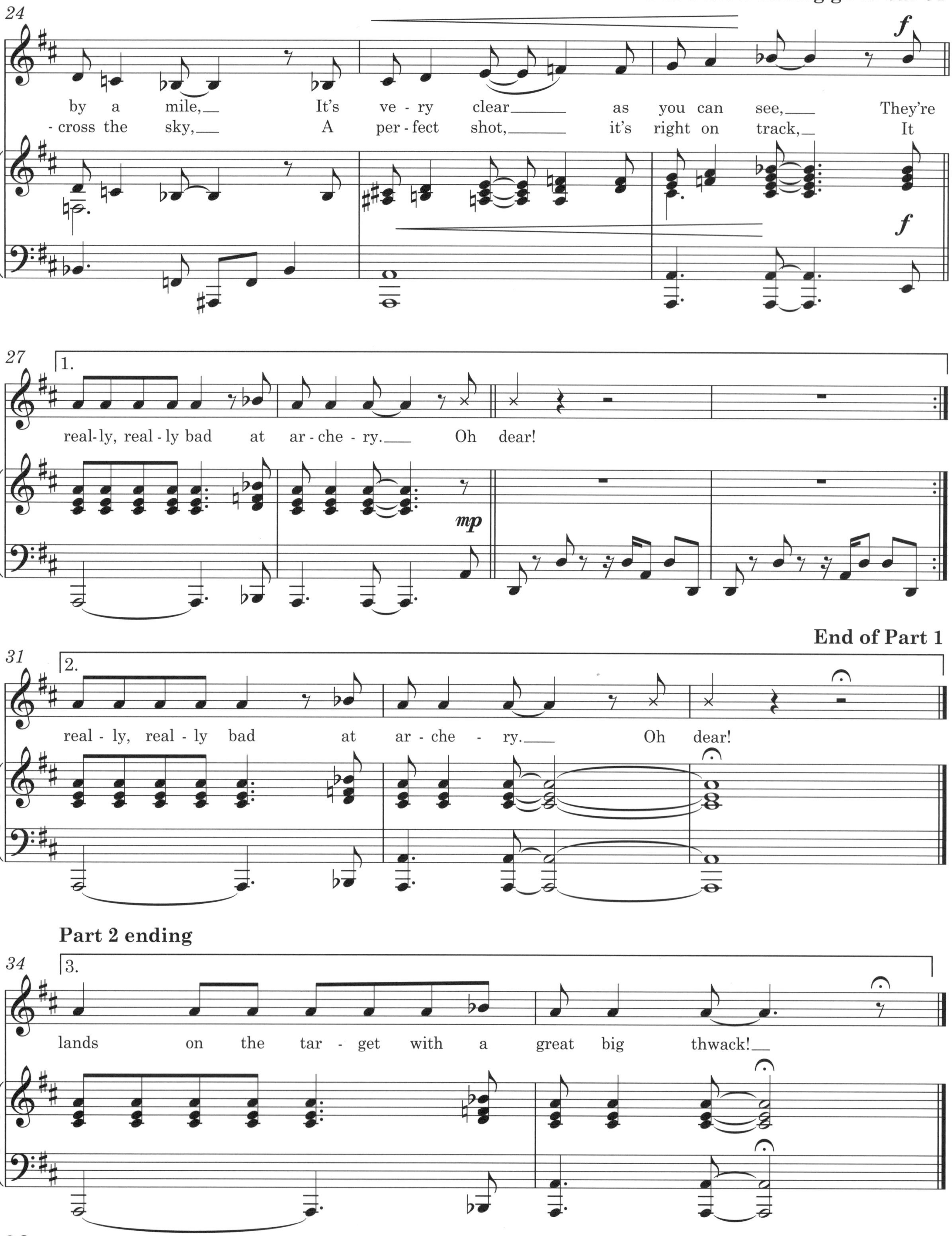
24
by a mile, It's ve - ry clear as you can see, They're
-cross the sky, A per - fect shot, it's right on track, It
f
f
27
1.
real-ly, real - ly bad at ar - che - ry. Oh dear!
mp
End of Part 1
31
2.
real - ly, real - ly bad at ar - che - ry. Oh dear!
Part 2 ending
34
3.
lands on the tar - get with a great big thwack!

Twang! Reprise

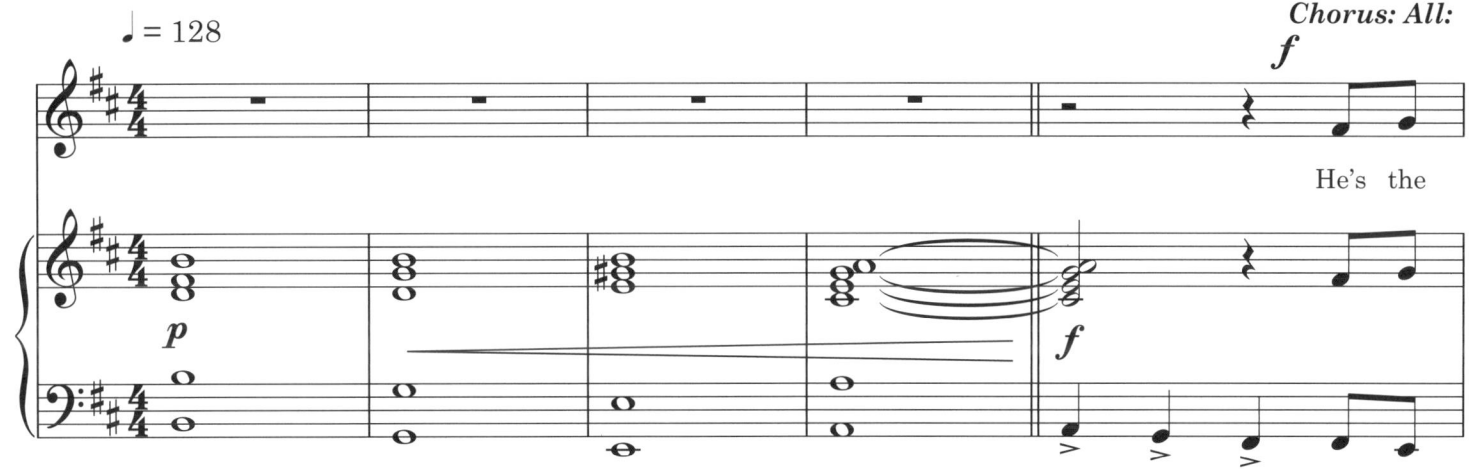

guy who goes twang - a - lang,___ The guy who goes twang!

And all the girls say, 'Hey! There goes a boy with
So just sit back while we tell you what you need to

style,_____ Got a hat with a fea - ther
know._____ A - bout the dude in the wood

and a real cute smile',_____ All the boys say, 'Hey man!
with the ar - row and bow,_____ It's a fact that a show should

We can be like him,
end up_____ with a bang,
If we spend more time
But our show ends
down at the gym!'
He's the
with a sim-ple twang,
oh yeah! Yes,
our show ends
with a sim-ple twang!

(small notes optional)

As a matter of fact, I been thinkin' about that. I think I got a way to flush 'im out.

Marion: Well, as long as Robin doesn't get sucked in.

Mensa: Ah, Robin'll be fine. He can look after 'imself.

Marion: I'm not so sure. Can you keep a secret?

Mensa: 'Course I can. What?

Marion: He's a rubbish archer.

Mensa: Well, I knows that. I'm a Wise Woman.

Marion: Oh. I thought I was the only one who knew.

Mensa: Nah. I seen 'im do that flashy invisible arrow routine. Never fooled me.

Marion: Weird, isn't it? How everyone goes along with it.

Mensa: Folks'll believe anythin' if it's packaged right.

Marion: I'm just worried that one day he won't pull it off and people will stop believing in him.

Mensa: I'll give you one of me lucky amulets if you like. Stick it round 'is neck. Keep bad fortune at bay.

Sarah: Does it work?

Mensa: Well, it's dipped in skunk oil, so it keeps pretty much everythin' at bay.

Marion: Thanks, but I'll pass. We've got to get moving before our heart rates drop.

Mensa: You can pass on a message from me, if you'd be so kind. Tell Robin ~ Read Between The Lines.

Marion: That's it?

Mensa: That's it.

Alice: What are you doing for the rest of the day, Mother Mensa?

Mensa: Oh, I got plans. A little visit I needs to make to a certain someone. Nice seein' you, girls.

Marion: You too.

Exit Marion and Marionettes.

Mensa: Lovely bunch o' lasses. Go far, they will, given half a chance to use their brains. Of course, all this superstitious nonsense don't help. *[Bites into a muffin, sits and begins stirring again]* Mice are nice in a cauldron, a cauldron, a cauldron…

23

Thunder. Linking music to next scene.

SCENE 5 ~ ROBIN'S CAMP

A fire is burning, over which a pot of forest stew is suspended. A jug of apple juice and four tankards are under a tree.

Forward to next track

Enter Allan.

Allan: Me again! I've been moving the song on, and want to run it past Robin. I've been following the smell of wood smoke, and there's a fire, right enough. But a lot of rough types hang out in Sherwood. How can I be sure this is the right den? *[Rap intro]* Uh-oh! Who's this coming?

Allan hides behind a tree. Enter Will, Little John and Much the Miller.

SONG ~ THE MERRY MEN RAP

All [whispered]: **Uh yeah! Yeah! Ohhh! Uh yeah! Yeah! Hey! Uh yeah! Yeah! Ohhh! Uh yeah! Yeah! Hey!**

Will [rapped]: **This is the den of the Mighty Merry Men, You are lookin' at the chosen few.**

Little John [rapped]: **If you're gonna live rough, Well you gotta be tough, With scars and the odd tattoo.**

Much [rapped]: **This world ain't good, but we in the wood, Gotta plan that might succeed,**

Will [rapped]: **We take the loot from the guy in the suit, And we give it to the guy in need.**

Chorus

All [sung]: **So here we are, the Merry Men, we hope you like our crew, We work for Rob, do a real good job, the best that we can do, We're big and strong, we right the wrong, we live on forest stew, We laugh and sing like anything, You are lookin' at the chosen few.**

Much [rapped]: **Now listen up and have some fun! Here come the names, one by one.**

Will [rapped]: **I'm Will! 'Nuf said! I'm the Scarlet dude and I dress in red.**

Little John [rapped]: **I'm John, big bloke. They call me little for a silly sort of joke.**

24

Much [rapped]: **I'm Much! I bake! They call me the Miller and I make a great cake.**

All [sung]: *Chorus*
So here we are...

The choir rhythmically chants the names of the three Merry Men. In turn, they come to the front to perform tough moves and poses (e.g. breakdancing, pretending to lift weights, baking in a macho manner).

All [rapped]: **Little John, Little John. Uh yeah! Yeah!**
Little John, Little John. Ohhh!
Will Scarlet. Uh yeah! Yeah!
Will Scarlet. Hey!
Much, Much. Uh yeah! Yeah!
Much, Much. Ohhh!
This is the den of the Mighty Merry Men,
You are lookin' at the chosen few.

All [sung]: *Chorus*
So here we are...

All [rapped]: **This is the den of the Mighty Merry Men,**
You are lookin' at the chosen few.

Forward to
next track

Enter Robin. Little John picks up the jug. The Merry Men and Robin pick up a tankard each.

Robin: You guys! Always kidding around.

Little John: Fermented apple juice, Rob?

Robin: Yes, why not? Fill 'er up, Little John.

Little John: Will? You?

Will: I will, yes.

Little John tops up the drinks. Much puts his hand over his tankard.

Little John: You too, Much?

Much: No, I've already had too much. I think it's past the sell-by date.

Little John: Well, it is medieval.

Much: It's got pips in. They stick in my teeth.

Little John: Faddy. Isn't he, Rob? The Miller's faddy.

Robin: Hey, hey! No name calling! Jokes and jolly banter only, if you please. A toast! To me and my crew!

Merry Men: To us! *[They drink.]*

Robin: A good day's work, lads. Three bags of gold and a horse. By the way, has anyone seen the horse?

Little John whistles.

25

Forward to next track

Little John:	Hey, horse! Are you there?

Sound effect of clopping and offstage whinny.

Little John:	He's there.

Allan emerges from behind a tree.

Allan:	*[to audience]* This is my big moment. I'm feeling a bit nervous, actually. Wish me luck.

Allan approaches Robin.

Allan:	Ahem. Er ~ excuse me.
Robin:	Oh. It's you.
Allan:	Yes. I followed the smell of wood smoke, like you said. I've come to run the song past you.
Merry Men:	Song?
Robin:	He's writing a song about me. He's a bard. His name's Allan-a-Dale.
Will:	What sort of music do you play, Al?
Allan:	Folk music, of course.
Much:	Not cool. Robin needs a cool song.
Little John:	Heavy metal. That's cool.
Robin:	Not to everybody, Little John. Go on, Allan. I'm listening.
Allan:	Thank you, Robin. Right then, here it is. *[Strums discord, opens mouth to sing, but is again interrupted.]*
Marion:	*[offstage]* Robin! Hey, Robin!
Allan:	*[to audience]* Would you believe it? Every time!

Enter Marion and the Marionettes.

Robin:	Hey, Marion.
Marion:	Hey, Robin.
Merry Men:	Hey, girls!
Marionettes:	Hey, guys!

They high five.

Robin:	*[to Marion]* Did you see the horse?
Marion:	No.
Robin:	Well there is one. Stole it this morning.
Alice:	Invisible, like your arrows.

26

Robin:	What about the new Wanted posters? They're all over the wood. I saved you one.
Marion:	No thanks, they make your nose look big. Actually, I've just called in with a message from Mensa.
Robin:	What ~ the Wise Woman?
Marion:	That's her. She says to tell you to Read Between The Lines.
Robin:	Hmm. There's nothing between lines but spaces. Where's the sense in that?
Marion:	It means you have to think beyond the words. Try and see what lies behind them.
Robin:	Ah. Right. *[to audience]* She's quite brainy, actually. I should listen to her more.

Friar Tuck enters at a run.

Friar Tuck:	Robin! Saints be praised! There you are!
Robin:	What's up, Friar?
Friar Tuck:	Terrible news! I've just come from the village! Prince John has doubled the taxes!
All:	No!
Friar Tuck:	Yes! And the new Sheriff's threatening to burn the huts!
All:	No!
Friar Tuck:	Yes! And Seth Poor and his wife have been arrested!
Much:	What ~ the Poor family?
Friar Tuck:	Yes! They're taking them to the jailhouse.
Little John:	What ~ Little Sammy too?
Friar Tuck:	Yes!
Marion:	Something must be done!
Robin:	Something must be done!
Alice:	She just said that.
Robin:	Said what? Look, sorry, girls, but I'm busy right now. We men have a problem that needs sorting out.
Little John:	When I think of that dear, innocent little boy. *[snivels]*
Robin:	Save your tears, Little John. We shall not pause before we rescue the poor pauper Poors from the poorhouse.
Will:	Don't you mean the jailhouse?
Robin:	Whatever.

Much:	But how? It's heavily guarded night and day.
Robin:	We'll storm it. Stout hearts will win the day.
Merry Men:	Right!
Marion:	It'd make more sense to stage an ambush in the forest. That way, you'll only have a handful of guards to deal with.

A long silence. The Marionettes nod supportively and wait for the reaction. There is none. It is as though she never spoke. Sound effect of wind blowing tumbleweed.

Robin:	Better still, we could stage an ambush before they get put in the slammer.
Merry Men:	Excellent! Brilliant! Good plan, Robin!
Robin:	Men! Follow me! We'll take the horse!

He bounds out, followed by the Merry Men and Friar Tuck.

| Allan: | Wait for me! *[to audience]* Looks like there's about to be some action. I need to be on the spot. |

Exit Allan.

| Marion: | *[shouts]* What about us? |
| Marion: | Ooh! Is my patience wearing thin! |

Sound effect of clopping and an offstage whinny, then silence. Linking music to next scene.

SCENE 6 ~ THE AMBUSH

A forest glade. There is a sound effect of clopping and an offstage whinny. Robin bounds in, followed by the Merry Men and Friar Tuck, all armed with sticks.

| Robin: | Quick, men! Hide yourselves! They're coming! |

They hide behind trees and bushes. Enter Allan, at a run, shouting.

Allan:	Hello? Robin? Yoo-hoo! Where is everyone?
Robin:	Allan, will you kindly get out of sight before you ruin everything!
Allan:	What?
Robin:	Get down! Oh, get him, Friar.

Friar Tuck yanks Allan behind a tree, just in time. Enter the Guards, roughly manhandling the Poor family.

Guard 1:	Get a move on, you lazy layabouts!
Little Sammy:	I can't! My little toesies is hurtin'!
Meg:	Stop dragging him, he's only small.
Little Sammy:	Boo-hoo, the nasty men. *[weeps]*

Seth: You should be ashamed of yourselves. If King Richard was here, he'd put a stop to your thuggery.

Guard 2: Well, he ain't.

Guard 3: Prince John's in charge now.

Guard 4: Anyway, we answers to the Sheriff.

Guard 5: Stop yer whining or it'll be the worst for you…

Robin: Unhand those people!

Robin bounds forward, brandishing his stick. The Merry Men and Friar Tuck jump out, sticks raised. Allan peeps fearfully from behind the tree. The Poors move out of the way.

Guard 1: Oh, my days! It's Hood!

SONG ~ AMBUSH SONG

Robin's gang and the Guards face up to each other. Robin's gang are banging their sticks on the ground in time. Intro of stick rhythms.

Chorus 1 (Merry Men):
Let the fight begin! We can't wait for it!
Wipe the floor with you, knock you round a bit!

Robin and his Merry Men surround the nervous Guards in a circle.

Merry Men:
Run along back to your mothers,
Hide behind your baby brothers,
We know our fighting is superior,
And we can't wait to knock you down!

Chorus 2 (Guards):
Please don't hurt us! Please don't blame us!
Wasn't our fault, someone made us!

Guards:
Though we come across as yobs, guv,
Bear in mind there ain't no jobs, guv.
Oh please show us mercy, let us run away,
And we'll head for some far-off town.

Chorus 1 and 2 together.

Greensleeves instrumental. The Guards try to escape and are recaptured by Robin and the Merry Men. There is much stick waving and struggling. The Guards are getting the worst of it. The Poors look on, shouting encouragement. Allan remains cowering behind his tree. The Guards are finally bested.

Chorus 1 and 2 together.

Coda of stick rhythms from the triumphant Merry Men.

Robin: Drop your weapons!

Forward to next track

The Guards look at each other, shamefaced, and drop their sticks.

Guard 1: Look, sorry. All right?

Guard 2: Didn't mean it.

Guard 3: Didn't want to.

Guard 4: No. Didn't.

Guard 5: Yeah. Sorry.

Robin: Apologise to *them*, not me.

Guards: *[to the Poors]* Sorry.

Little John: Not sorry enough, though. Robin? I'm taking them back home and I'm telling their mums. Okay with you?

Robin: Be my guest, Little John.

Little John marches the drooping Guards offstage.

Robin: Another good day's work, lads. *[High fives the Merry Men.]*

Meg: Oh, Robin ~ we can't thank you enough.

Seth: Our saviour. *[Wrings Robin's hand.]*

Robin: All part of the service. Much! Friar! These good people shall ride home in style. Fetch the horse.

Meg: What horse?

Robin, Much, Will and Friar Tuck whistle. Sound effect of clopping and an offstage whinny.

Much: That horse. Come on!

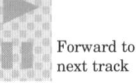

Forward to next track

Much and Friar Tuck lead the Poors offstage.

Little Sammy: Ooh! Hooray! A ride on a horsie!

Robin: *[to audience]* He is kind of annoying.

Allan sheepishly comes out of hiding.

Robin: Ah. There you are, Allan. Get a good view, did you? From behind that tree?

Allan: Sorry. I'm just not good at violence.

Robin: So it would seem.

Allan: It was a great fight, though. I'll put it into the song, of course.

Robin: Don't bother. I think you proved your worth today.

Will: Yeah. Come on, Rob, let's go home.

Exit Robin and Will, leaving Allan awash with shame.

Allan: *[to audience]* I feel terrible. I've let him down. I didn't

30

realise I was such a coward until now. *[sighs]* Oh well. What's done is done. I suppose I'll just try and move the song on. Although I don't suppose he'll want to hear it.

Allan trails out sadly. Linking music to next scene.

Forward to next track

SCENE 7 ~ PRINCE JOHN'S THRONE ROOM

A fanfare plays. Prince John is on his throne with his Guards at his side. He is talking to the Sheriff.

Prince John:	What? A ham bush, did you say?
Sheriff:	Yes!
Prince John:	I'm guessing some sort of ~ bacon tree?
Sheriff:	No. Ambush! Where you get jumped on and all your prisoners get stolen.
Prince John:	And you let this happen?
Sheriff:	I wasn't even there. It's not my fault. It's Hood! He's getting bolder by the minute.
Prince John:	Who? Hood? Hood who?
Sheriff:	That wretched Robin of Loxley. Calls himself Robin Hood. Hangs out in Sherwood Forest with a gang of outlaws. Robs the rich to feed the poor.
Prince John:	Good grief. That is *so* not on.
Sheriff:	He's got it all going for him. Got quite a following. Young, handsome, brave, smells nice, shoots arrows so fast they're invisible...
Prince John:	Enough. I don't like him. String him up, and that's an order.
Sheriff:	Easier said than done. He's in hiding.
Prince John:	Well, flush him out.
Sheriff:	Have you seen the size of Sherwood Forest?
Prince John:	Do it, or I'll take your badge away.
Sheriff:	Not that! Anything but that!
Prince John:	Well, come up with a plan, then. I'm not having these kind of people wandering around, whipping up trouble.

Enter Fishy.

Fishy:	Excuse me, sire. There's a Wise Woman at the door. She claims to have seen your future in the jars.
Prince John:	Don't you mean stars?
Fishy:	No, she definitely said jars.

31

Forward to next track

Prince John: Intriguing. Well, show her in, then. We'll take a little break here, Sheriff. I want to hear all about my glorious future.

Fishy: *[shouts]* All right, in you come!

Sound of thunder. Enter Mensa. She has a basket full of nasty looking jars over her arm. Prince John starts, trembles and reaches for Fishy's hand.

Mensa: Mornin', yer princeness. I'm Mensa, the Wise Woman. I've brought me mystic jars. Where shall I put 'em?

Fishy: Not there! That's a polished table, you foolish old woman!

Mensa: Ooh. Hoity-toity. You won't be so snotty when I tells you what I sees in 'em.

Prince John: Well, all I can see in them is what looks like ~ EEK! Boiled mice. *[Flinches and cowers. Fishy pats him absently.]*

Fishy: There, there, sire.

Prince John: Why can't she just make jam, like most old women?

Mensa: Oh, you don't wanna look in *them*. Them's for common people. I uses a special jar for royalty.

She reaches into her gown and brings out an ornate silver jar with a crown on the label.

Sheriff: What's in that?

Mensa: Strange things. Mysterious things. Powdered unicorn horn. Rainbow drops. Pixie droppin's. Altogether better class of ingredient.

Prince John: Go on, then. Tell me what you see.

Mensa: Wisdom don't come free. You'll have to cross me palm with silver.

Prince John: Sheriff. Pay the woman.

The Sheriff reluctantly gives Mensa a coin. She pockets it.

Mensa: Now then. We shall see what we shall see.

SONG ~ TIME TO BE HYPNOTISED

Mensa unscrews the cap. During the song, she moves around the stage, waving the jar and making mysterious hand passes. Prince John, Fishy and the Sheriff's eyes begin to droop as the song begins.

Mensa:
Time now to close your eyes, time to be hypnotised.
All now will be revealed, just keep your eyelids sealed.

Forward to next track

Chorus
**I see you on a sunny day, in a meadow far away,
Heading for a future where all will be well.**

**Warm wind and sky of blue, everyone loving you,
Everyone cheering you, nobody jeering you.**

Chorus
I see you on a sunny day...

**Now I can clearly see, a contest of archery.
Here in your hand you hold, an arrow of solid gold.**

**I see you on a sunny day, in a meadow far away,
Heading for the future and here ends my spell...**

Mensa: Remember! Archery contest!

Snaps fingers. Prince John, the Sheriff and Fishy come to.

Prince John: Think I dropped off there for a moment.

Sheriff: Me too.

Fishy: Yes, it's uncomfortably warm in here. All right, old hag, you've had your moment, time's up. Out! Shoo!

Exit Mensa. Sound effect of thunder.

Forward to next track

Prince John: Now, what were we talking about?

Sheriff: Robin of Loxley. And funnily enough, I've had a rather good idea about how to flush him out.

Prince John: It doesn't involve, by any chance ~ an archery tournament?

Sheriff: Well... yes.

Prince John: Amazing! I had the very same thought.

Fishy: Funnily enough, so did I.

Prince John: But I had it first, which makes me the cleverest. My idea is to hold a great tournament and invite all the best archers in the land. I myself shall graciously present the prize, which will be a golden arrow.

Sheriff: Hood won't be able to resist entering. Fan pressure, apart from anything else.

Fishy: Then, when he comes forward to claim the prize, you can arrest him on the spot.

Sheriff: My pleasure! When shall we do it?

Prince John: Next Saturday, in the grounds of your castle. I shall be staying with you.

Sheriff: Oh.

Prince John:	I shall require mead-making facilities and a trouser press. Fishy, issue a proclamation. Then start packing.
Fishy:	What... now?
Prince John:	Certainly. I shall be taking my entire wardrobe and the royal treasure chest. These peasants need to see who's boss 'round here. I shall ride in a palanquin. Flash the cash. Dazzle them with my glitzy lifestyle.
Fishy:	Is that wise? You're not too popular right now.
Prince John:	Nonsense. I am the almost-any-day-now king. I shall show off accordingly. Go!

Exit Fishy.

Prince John:	And bring the bling! *[to Sheriff]* And you ~ get back home and make preparations. *[exit Sheriff]* Huh! Robin Hood indeed!

Linking music to next scene.

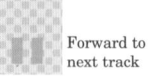

SCENE 8 ~ ROBIN'S CAMP

Robin, the Merry Men, Marion and the Marionettes are gathered around the fire. Allan is skulking behind a bush at the side of the stage. He speaks confidentially to the audience.

Allan:	Hey! I'm over here! After disgracing myself at the ambush, I'm not sure Robin wants to see me. I can't help hanging around the camp, though. Just in case he changes his mind and wants to hear the song. I could play you a bit now, before something else happens to stop me. It goes like this... *[chord]*

Enter Friar Tuck, with parchment.

Will:	Hey Friar! What's happenin'?
Allan:	That's it. I give up.
Much:	Did you see the horse?
Friar Tuck:	What? No.
Robin:	Has anyone seen the horse?

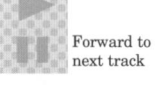

Little John whistles. Sound effect of clopping and an offstage whinny.

All:	He's there.
Friar Tuck:	I thought you might be interested in this. *[hands Robin the parchment]* Your sort of thing, I imagine.

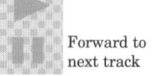

Robin reads the parchment. Sound of thunder.

Mensa:	*[offstage]* Remember! Read Between The Lines!
Robin:	*[to Marion]* Can you read this?

34

Marion:	*[takes it]* Oh. Oh dear.
Robin:	What?
Marion:	An archery contest, to be held on Saturday in the grounds of the Sheriff's castle. Prince John is to award the winner with a golden arrow.
Robin:	Oh. Really? *[to audience]* Tricky. How do I get out of this one?
Marion:	It's a trap, of course. They know you won't be able to resist entering. They want to lure you there, then pounce!

Silence. The Marionettes wait with bated breath. Sound effect of wind blowing tumbleweed.

Robin:	You know, I've been thinking. This could be a trap. They probably want to lure me there, then pounce.
Much:	He's right, you know.
Little John:	No flies on Robin.
Robin:	Probably best if I don't go.
Will:	Huh? Are you crazy? You've got to show up, Rob. You can't let your fans down.
Marion:	Of course, there might be a way round it. You could go along in disguise.

Sound effect of wind blowing tumbleweed.

Robin:	Of course, there could be a way around it. Maybe some sort of disguise. Guys, just give me a moment will you? I need to think. *[walks centre stage and addresses the audience]* Now I'm in trouble. Yes, I can go in disguise. But I've got to win too. Invisible archery won't cut it this time. Not with proper rules and a real target. This time, it's all about skill. What to do, what to do?

Allan sadly plays a discord at the side of the stage. Robin notices him.

Robin:	Allan?
Allan:	Yes, Robin?
Robin:	Come with me. I'd like a private word.

They walk offstage, Robin whispering in Allan's ear. Linking music to next scene.

SCENE 9 ~ THE CONTEST

Prince John processes through the audience. His brimming treasure chest follows behind on a stretcher carried by Guards. He is accompanied by Fishy. At the same time, the stage fills with everyone who has turned out for the contest: the Villagers, the Poors, Marion, the Marionettes, the Merry Men, Friar Tuck, Mensa and the competing archers. Some are carrying flags to add to

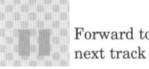

the festive air ~ although people don't look too happy. The Sheriff is there to greet Prince John. Little Sammy carries a target.

Forward to next track

SONG ~ HE'S RICH [PART 1]

> *All:*
> **Rich, rich, rich, rich, rich! Rich, rich, rich, rich, rich!**
> **Rich, rich, rich, rich, rich, rich, rich, rich.**
>
> **He's rich! Prince John is rich! [Rich x 13]**
> **He's stinking, stinking rich!**
> **His treasure chest is full to overflowing,**
> **He's rich! Prince John is rich! [Rich x 13]**
> **He's stinking, stinking rich!**
> **How rich he is, we have no way of knowing,**
> **He's rich! Prince John is rich! [Rich x 5]**
>
> **His gowns are trimmed with furry baby foxes,**
> **His crowns are always spilling out of boxes,**
> **He's loads of gold and jewels by the score,**
> **But he's always wanting more and more,**
> **He's rich, he's stinking rich!**
>
> **Rich, rich, rich...**

Forward to next track

Prince John: Halt!

The procession comes to a halt.

Prince John: What's that ghastly old ruin up ahead, Fishy?

Fishy: The Sheriff's castle, sire. You did say to give him one of the crumbly ones.

Prince John: Yes, but I didn't expect to be staying there. Good grief. Who'd be a king?

Fishy: You would.

Prince John: How true. Move on!

The procession moves on, to part 2 of the song, which is sung more aggressively. The onstage actors are pointing to the oncoming procession. There is some fist-waving. Little Sammy sets up the target at the back of the hall, behind the audience.

SONG ~ HE'S RICH [PART 2]

> *All:*
> **Rich, rich, rich, rich, rich! Rich, rich, rich, rich, rich!**
> **Rich, rich, rich, rich, rich, rich, rich, rich.**
>
> **He's rich! Prince John is rich! [Rich x 13]**
> **He's stinking, stinking rich!**
> **You've never ever seen a man so greedy,**

36

He's rich! Prince John is rich! [Rich x 13]
He's stinking, stinking rich!
He doesn't give a fig about the needy,
He's rich, Prince John is rich! [Rich x 5]

We disapprove of how he made his money,
His ruthless methods aren't the least bit funny,
He'll be expecting us to clap and cheer,
But he'll get a poor reception here,
He's rich! Prince John is rich! [Rich x 5]

We're poor, poor, poor, [Rich x 5]
We're poor, poor, poor, [Rich x 8]
We're poor, poor, poor and he's rich!
He's stinking rich!

Forward to next track

Prince John and his cavalcade arrive onstage.

Sheriff: *[bowing]* Your highness! Welcome to my humble castle. Let's give a big Nottingham welcome to Prince John!

Angry muttering from the crowd. A few boos.

Prince John: I'm sensing a little disrespect here.

Sheriff: Just a few rough elements, sire. They'll cheer up when the archery begins.

Meg: Long live King Richard!

Seth: Down with Prince John!

Prince John: Who said that?

Sheriff: Ignore them. Please ~ be seated.

Prince John, Fishy and the cavalcade walk to the podium. The treasure chest is placed to one side.

Prince John: Not even a cushion for the royal behind. Typical. *[He sits.]*

Sheriff: *[addressing the crowd]* Right, everybody, lighten up and that's an order. This is a happy occasion. Wave your flags or I'll set the guards on you.

Fishy: Shall I do the honours, sire?

Prince John: Yes, yes. I'd like to get home sometime this week.

Fishy: I declare this archery contest open!

Sheriff: *[to the crowd]* Enthusiasm! Now!

All: Hooray!

Fishy: Will the contestants line up, facing the target.

The archers line up, facing the audience.

Fishy: The man who comes nearest the bull's-eye will be declared the winner of the golden arrow.

Everyone looks at Prince John expectantly.

Prince John: What? Oh, right, yes. This. *[He holds up the golden arrow.]*

Sheriff: Admiration! Now!

All: Oooooh.

Fishy: Take aim ~ ready ~

The following song needs some choreographed movements. Everyone can be aiming their bows and firing imaginary arrows, as well as pretending to duck and dive.

SONG ~ THE ARROW'S IN THE AIR [PART ONE]

Four archers step up and prepare to fire arrows.

All:
**Up a bit, down a bit, left a bit, aim for the
     bull's-eye.
Up a bit, down a bit, right a bit,
This arrow's gonna fly ~ fire!**

Chorus
**The arrow's in the air, the arrow's in the air,
We've got to duck and dodge it as it rises into
     orbit.
The arrow's in the air, the arrow's in the air,
It's spinning round and round, and heading back
     to ground.**

**They have no skill, they have no style,
They've missed the target by a mile,
It's very clear as you can see,
They're really, really bad at archery. Oh dear!**

The next four archers step up and prepare to fire.

(Repeat The Arrow's in the Air song.)

Prince John: Well, that was appalling. I thought they were supposed to be great archers.

Fishy: A poor show indeed. Nobody else want a try?

Marion: I'll have a go!

Prince John: Ah me, the nonsense talked by girls. Run along, dear, and see if you can rustle up some tea. Proceed, Fishy.

The Marionettes hold back Marion, who is raging. They form a huddle. They are hatching a plan to steal the treasure chest.

Fishy: Thank you. Now, are there any more real men who wish to try their luck?

Robin: *[offstage, in a quavering voice]* Me! I would!

Enter a figure that everyone onstage thinks is Robin, disguised as an old man. He has a hooded

cloak, a long grey beard, and a bow and quiver. Excited muttering from the crowd, who part to make way. In fact, it is Allan, finally getting his minute of fame.

Friar Tuck:	It's Robin!
Little John:	Yep. Here comes our boy!
Will:	Leaving it to the last minute, as usual.
Much:	Great disguise, eh?
Prince John:	*[to Fishy]* It's him, isn't it? It's Hood. Is it?
Fishy:	Sssh. Act normal, sire.
Sheriff:	And who might you be, greybeard?
Allan:	*[old man's voice]* They call me Old Kevin. I may be getting on, but I was a fine shot in my youth.

Fishy, the Sheriff and Prince John exchange pantomime winks.

Prince John:	Indeed? Well, Old Kevin, let us see if your trembling hand and ancient eyes can still cut it.

'Old Kevin' takes centre stage.

Allan:	Now, let me see. How does it go again?

SONG ~ THE ARROW'S IN THE AIR [PART 2]

All:
**Up a bit, down a bit, left a bit, aim for the
    bull's-eye.
Up a bit, down a bit, right a bit,
This arrow's gonna fly ~ fire!**

Chorus
**The arrow's in the air, the arrow's in the air,
It's flying straight and true,
Which is what it's s'posed to do.
The arrow's in the air, the arrow's in the air,
A perfect demonstration, we're full of admiration.**

**It flies so true, it flies so high, accelerates across
    the sky,
A perfect shot, it's right on track,
It lands on the target with a great big thwack!**

All:	Woo-hoo! Yeah!
Little Sammy:	*[from the back]* Bull's-eye! Slap bang in the middle!

He runs to the stage carrying the target, which has an arrow sticking out of it. He shows it to the Sheriff and Prince John. The cast surge forward and gather around 'Old Kevin', clapping him on the back.

Prince John:	Good lord. Will you look at that!
Sheriff:	Sheer luck. The wind was in his favour.

Forward to
next track

39

Fishy:	[meaningfully] I think he deserves the golden arrow, though, don't you?
Sheriff:	Oh yes. Of course. Old Kevin, step forward.

The crowd parts and 'Old Kevin' hobbles to the podium. Prince John stands.

Prince John:	I have great pleasure in presenting you with this wonderful golden arrow, Old Kevin. Or should I say ~ Robin Hood!

He leans forward and snatches back the hood of the cloak, to reveal ~ Allan!

Sheriff:	This isn't him! It isn't Hood!
Little John:	He's right! It's not!
Will:	It's that idiot singer. I don't get it. Where's Rob?
Much:	Search me!
Prince John:	Who is it, then?
Sheriff:	I haven't a clue. Who are you?
Allan:	They call me Allan-a-Dale.
Prince John:	Why are you passing yourself off as Old Kevin?
Fishy:	And why are you wearing a false beard?
Allan:	Why not? There's no law against it.
Prince John:	There is now. No old man impersonations or fake weird beardery allowed, by order of the king!
All:	Boooo! Siddown!
Meg:	You're not king yet!
Prince John:	Who said that!
Allan:	In the meantime, I claim the golden arrow!
Sheriff:	I'm not so sure about that.
Marion:	For shame! Give Allan the arrow!
All:	Yes! Give him the arrow. Allan, Allan, Allan!
Sheriff:	All right!

Allan gets the arrow and passes it round to be admired. People crowd around him, congratulating him. Marion, the Marionettes, Mensa and the Merry Men form a huddle.

Little John:	I still don't get it. This isn't the way it's supposed to happen. Robin's supposed to win.
Will:	He did.
All:	What?
Will:	Think about it. There's no way that fool Allan could have

pulled off that shot. Only Rob could do that.

Much: You're right. It's a trick. Come on, Marion, he's in hiding somewhere around here isn't he? You must know.

Marion: I haven't a clue. For once, he's done something quite clever that I didn't think of first.

Mensa: Dunno why you're all standin' around natterin'. There's a treasure chest over there, ripe for the takin'.

Little John: Ooh. She's right. Come on, boys.

Marion: Hold it! Why should you have all the fun? This is a job for the girls.

Prince John: Sheriff? A word.

He stands and pokes the Sheriff in the chest, propelling him backwards and away from the treasure chest. While he berates the Sheriff, Marion and the Marionettes quietly make off with the chest.

Prince John: I am not happy, Sheriff. You have brought me here under false pretences. You told me we would arrest Hood! This is your fault.

Sheriff: Me? Why me? We all came up with the same idea.

Fishy suddenly notices the space where the chest once was.

Fishy: Er ~ sire?

Prince John: Go away, Fishy. *[to Sheriff]* Of course it's your fault. I've a good mind to take your badge away right now!

Fishy: Sire!

Prince John: What?

Fishy points to the space where the chest was. Marion and the Marionettes re-enter, whistling innocently.

Prince John: My chest! Someone's stolen my treasure chest! Can things get any worse?

Sound effect of a fanfare, followed by kingly music.

All: It's King Richard! Long live the King!

Prince John: Uh-oh.

King Richard enters. Everyone bows and curtsies.

King Richard: Yes, yes, here I am. Back at last from the crusades. Wheeled in at the very end, as usual. It's a thankless role, but at least I get a good costume. A big hand for the costume, if you please. *[waits for the clapping to die down]* All right, simmer down, it's time for the knighting. *[to Prince John, who is trying to sneak away]* Hold it right there, brother. I'll deal with you later. First things first.

Forward to next track

41

Step forward, Robin Hood! Is he here? Where is that son of a gun!

Cheers from the crowd as Robin enters, happy and grinning.

Little John: Here he is! I knew he wouldn't be far away! Hey, Rob! How did you pull off that trick shot?

Will: Sssh! The King's talking.

King Richard: I've been hearing good things about you, Hood. And us proper kings like to reward loyalty. Kneel.

He unsheathes his sword. Kingly music as Robin is knighted.

King Richard: Arise, Sir Robin of Loxley!

More congratulations as people flock to Robin.

Robin: Hey. Thanks, guys. Thanks a lot. There's just one more thing to tick off on today's Good Deed list. And that's ~ marryin' Marion.

General laughter at Robin's 'hilarious' pun.

Marion: I beg your pardon? I'm on a list?

Robin: *[ignoring her]* Yep. I think I just might marry her. Right now.

Alice: Don't bank on it. She might have something to say about that.

Susan: She's got plenty to say about lots of things, if only you'd listen.

Phoebe: You never hear a word she says.

Lizzie: You just talk over her.

Sarah: That's right, you do.

Robin: *[to Marion]* Do I?

Marion: Yes, you do.

Robin: Well, I'm very sorry. Would a bunch of flowers help?

Robin clicks his fingers. A bunch of flowers is passed out from the wings and handed along to Robin, who presents it with a flourish. Marion throws it over her shoulder.

Marion: It'll take more than that. We've got some talking to do, Robin.

Alice: Yes. How come your gang has only boys in?

Robin: I don't know. I wasn't thinking. You can join if you like.

Susan: What, to make the tea?

Robin: No, no. You can do whatever you like. Swig apple juice.

42

Ride the horse. Anything.

Allan: Robin?

Robin: Yes, Allan?

Allan: Can I sing my song now?

Robin: Not a good time, Allan.

Allan: But I've spent hours and hours on it. It presents your life in great detail. All the background history, your noble deeds, your politics, that invisible archery scam that everyone gets taken in by...

Mensa steps forward and put her hand over his mouth.

Mensa: Ah, they don't want to 'ear all that again. There's only one thing they needs to know about Robin.

SONG ~ TWANG! (REPRISE)

Chorus (all):
He's the guy who goes twang! Twang!
He's the guy who goes twang! Twang-a-lang!
He's the guy who goes twang! Twang!
He's the guy who goes twang! Twang-a-lang!

And he lived long ago with an arrow and bow
In an outlaw gang! [What a gang!]
He wore a suit of lovely Lincoln Green,
Like a medieval model in a magazine,
That dude called Robin Hood,
He's the guy who goes twang-a-lang,
The guy who goes twang!

And all the girls say, 'Hey! There goes a boy with
    style,
Got a hat with a feather and a real cute smile.'
All the boys say, 'Hey man! We can be like him,
If we spend more time down at the gym!'

Chorus
He's the guy who goes twang! Twang!...

He can swing through the trees with the greatest
    of ease,
Like an orang-utan! [Orang-utan!]
He wore a suit of lovely Lincoln Green,
Like a medieval model in a magazine,
That dude called Robin Hood,
He's the guy who goes twang-a-lang,
The guy who goes twang!

So just sit back while we tell you what you need to
    know,

43

**About the dude in the wood with the arrow and
    bow,
It's a fact that a show should end up with a bang,
But our show ends with a simple twang, oh yeah!
Yes, our show ends with a simple twang!**

Applause. Mensa conducts the curtain call.

Mensa: Ladies and gents ~ give it up for the Singin' Chorus!
         The Guards!
         The Villagers!
         The Poor family!
         The Marionettes!
         King Richard!
         Lord Fishy!
         Prince John!
         The Sheriff of Nottingham!
         Friar Tuck!
         Little John!
         Will Scarlett!
         Much the Miller!
         Allan-a-Dale!
         Maid Marion!
         Robin Hood!
         Me!
         And a big hand for the invisible 'orse!

Sound effect of clopping and an offstage whinny.

THE END